Essays on Evolution

Geoffrey Ponder

Geoffrey Ponder
Copyright © 2018 Geoffrey Ponder

ISBN: 1985717565

ISBN-13: 978-1985717565

Evolution Essays

DEDICATION

4

This book is dedicated to Josie Adler, my Godmother

CONTENTS

Geoffrey Ponder

Geoffrey Ponder

ACKNOWLEDGMENTS

Thanks to all the teachers (in the broader sense of the word) who stimulated the Biological Evolution class.

Evaluating Phylogeny Analysis

The purpose of this exercise was to get a better understanding of how we can use different methods to determine the phylogeny of a species. Several methods were used to evaluate how each can illustrate the likely evolutionary inheritance of a group of related organisms.

Aims of the Phylogeny Exercise

This exercise has several fundamental aims. The first is to get a better understanding of how the evolutionary relationships between a small set of organisms can be determined. This can be down using several methods, including making diagrams of proposed trees, or using software programs to process data that is input.

Secondly it is to be tested that the methods outlined above can be applied to both morphological and molecular data. By 'morphological' is meant characteristics of organisms which are evaluated as being sufficiently distinctive to be of significance. Molecular data relates to information which has been derived by more technical analyses.

The most likely phylogeny can be determined by identifying the most parsimonious evolutionary tree by making comparisons of alternative diagrams, or else by using an automated computer program which can also calculate the most parsimoneous phylogeny diagram.

Concepts of Phylogeny

A fundamental principle of Evolution is that any species has evolved from an earlier group of species from which it differs in significant ways. The most obvious differences are in physical appearance, although other differences will be more subtle such as type of food eaten, behaviour patterns, foods preferred, etc.

Usually two species are considered to be distinct if, however closely they resemble each other, they are not able to breed to produce offspring. Please note that this applies primarily to animals. Speciation in plants differs in other ways.

Consideration of the way that species have evolved from earlier species has brought about the concept of a Tree of Life. This shows the various various divergences from earlier species. With the passing of time a species is likely to branch (as shown in a pictorial manner) giving rise to two species that evolve with different modifications of certain features. Each of these species then itself branches. Over many millions of years multiple millions of various kinds of organisms have evolved from a single proposed organism at the base, or root, of the tree.

The way that the tree can show the path of evolution of species is not always easy to determine. Evolutionary biologists have needed to develop various methods for putting together a proposed tree of life. Mostly this is inferred from the study of living organisms rather than fossils.

When investigating the phylogeny of species, several fundamental principles will be assumed. The more similarities in appearance that two organisms have, we can assume the more closely related they are. Also the less time that has passed since the divergence of two organisms, then fewer evolutionary changes will have taken place.

As a fundamental concept in evolution, we accept that every species has come into existence coincident both in space and time with a closely allied species.

Potential Problems in Deriving Phylogeny

There are various potential difficulties when trying to outline the phylogeny of seemingly related organisms. For example, there might be a particular feature shared by both organisms, say wings in both birds and bats, but this feature was not actually present in their last common ancestor. This indicates that the feature evolved independently in each organism, so that the evolutionary relationship is not direct. If a feature is found in the last common ancestor of all related species, then we can assume that relatedness is indicated.

Determining Distinguishing Features in related Samples

For the purpose of this exercise, we made use of various luxury chocolates, with a variety of external appearance. Unfortunately only visual criteria, including whether the specimen is wrapped or not, could be used for the purposes of this exercise. It would have been highly useful if the taste-feature could have been included as a factor, but the overseer sternly warned me against taking a taste test and I assumed this was because he knew that the samples could be poisonous. (As it happens, I tested for this at the end of the formal session, and it turned out that in fact all specimens could have the 'Delicious' assessment assigned.)

We first needed to decide on the significant visual features which could be used for the differentiation of the chocolate samples. These features included whether the item had a light or dark colour, included a swirl or stripes, wrapped in foil, etc. Fortunately it turned out that although some features were shared between the samples, there were sufficiently distinctive differences in various factors for individual 'species' to be inferred.

Then, once a sufficient number of visual features had been decided upon, a table could be created showing whether the feature was a characteristic of each sample. A sample table is shown below. The number 0 indicates that the feature wasn't associated with the particular sample, while 1 indicates that the feature was associated.

Species	Camouflage stripes	(Loss of) silvery carapace	Elongate	Liquid haemolymph (filling)
	0	0	0	0
	1	1	0	0
	1	1	1	0
	0	1	0	1
	0	0	1	1

From this collection of data a cladogram (evolutionary tree without a timescale) can be put together. This is an attempt to map out the proposed relationships between the individual samples, trying to find the most likely evolutionary relationships and development sequences. An example of a cladogram is shown below, although it needs to be recognised that alternative diagrams are possible.

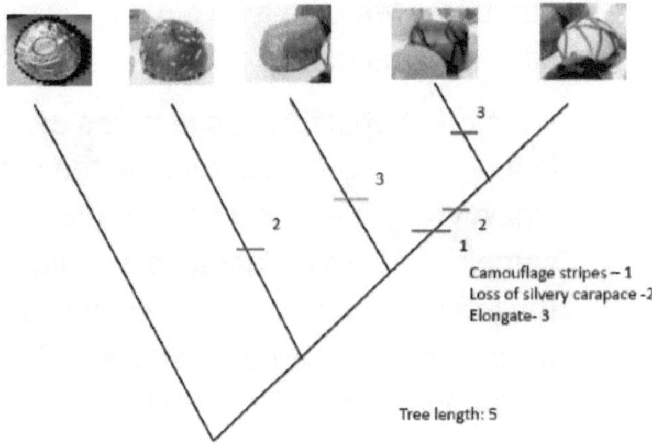

In this particular example, the chocolate samples are shown across the top and a proposed phylogeny outline is below. Because the sample at the very left is covered with foil, and the others are 'bare', it is shown as being separate from the rest. The two samples of the right both have camouflage stripes so they are shown as connected on the diagram. However the second from the right has been classified as elongated so it is on a separate branch than the only other sample which shares having camouflage stripes. When a selected sample is distinguishable from another sample which otherwise is similar, this is indicated by a short line across the branch and this short line is numbered with the type of classification which differentiates the two.

Note that different structures can be used in the cladogram, according to the order in which you put the branches to the different samples. The tree length is calculated from the total number of short lines which distinguish the different samples. This corresponds to the minimum number of evolutionary changes needed to fit each tree. It will probably be necessary to put together several trial trees to find the tree with the minimum tree length.

The reason why the tree with the least number of evolutionary changes is considered the best alternative, is because we are following the principle of parsimony. We are assuming that the most simple tree is most likely to correspond with the actual evolutionary outcome in real life, although this isn't necessarily the case. It would be interesting to see where this conclusion doesn't apply.

Putting Together a Cladogram using Molecular Data

The initial cladograms were put together using criteria obtained from visual

	1	2	3	4	5	6	7	8	9	10
F. rocheriensis	Cys	Ser	Asn	Ser	Ser	Thr	Cys	Met	Leu	Gly
T. horridfillingus	Cys	Ser	Leu	Leu	Ser	Thr	Cys	Val	Leu	Ser
T. subdeliciousus	Cys	Ser	Asn	Leu	Ser	Thr	Cys	Val	Leu	Ser
T.deliciousus	Cys	Gly	Leu	Leu	Ser	Thr	Cys	Met	Leu	Gly
T.lefttoendii	Cys	Ser	Leu	Leu	Ser	Thr	Cys	Val	Leu	Ser

observation. An alternative method of producing cladograms to indicate the phylogeny of a collection of species is to make use of molecular data. This data is obtained from more technical procedures, and is presented in the form of a table such as that shown below.

The new table based on the molecular data looks like this

Geoffrey Ponder

	1.	2.	3.	4.	5.	6.	7.	8.	9.	10
F. Rocheriensis	0	0	0	0	0	0	0	0	0	0
T. Horridfillingus.	0	0	110	0	0	10	1			
T. Subdeliciousus	0	0	0	1	0	0	0	1	0	1
T. Deliciousus.	0	1	1	1	0	0	0	0	0	0
T. Lefttoendi	0	0	1	0	0	0	1	0	1	1

The table made up from molecular data allows more complexity in types than the more basic factors taken from morphological data.

Using the Computer Package PAUP for Phylogenetic Analysis

Already cladograms have been produced using manual preparation of data, and then making actual diagrams. This is an acceptable use of human resources for small amounts of data, when limited numbers of species and significant characteristics are being evaluated.

However when many species are being considered, with large numbers of characteristics to be involved, then it is only practicable to make use of specialised computer programs. There are various alternatives available, with one of the better known and widely used being the PAUP package.

To be honest, PAUP is a somewhat basic package, with a very user-unfriendly front end. It is necessary to be very careful to enter the data on screens, making sure that all entries are exactly right otherwise the package won't even function. It is strange that although complicated processing is undertaken by the package, the front end is comparatively primitive.

The PAUP package had already been installed on laptop computers which were made available to us. After we were given an outline of how the package actually works, we were able to enter the necessary information and produce the reports. These reports show various potential analyses for the phylogeny of the species being considered.

The printout of the PAUP report is included as an Appendix. This shows different outcomes according to the way they variables involved were handled.

Summing up Findings of the Phylogeny Exercise

Although for a newcomer to this aspect of evolution, getting a reasonable understanding of phylogenic analysis was initially quite difficult. However when detailed instructions had been absorbed, and test analyses carried out, the elements of the analytical procedure became clearer.

Although usually such analyses would only be done taking advantage of the extensive processing power of computers, it was useful for manual breakdown to be carried out in order for a better understanding of the fundamental principles to be gained.

Most importantly of all, we learned of the key principle of parsimony. Basically this means that although various analyses can be produced, usually the preferable analysis will be the simpler when fewer potential pathways are included in the cladogram. This is more likely to reflect the actual real-life situation when evolution of various related species is taking place.

Also it became clearer that phylogenetic analysis plays a crucial part of the study of evolution as it helps give a much better idea of how any particular species actually evolved over an extended period of time.

Works Referenced

Archibald, John **One plus One equals One** Oxford University Press, 2014

Dawkins, Richard **A Devil's Chaplain** Weidenfeld and Nicolson, 2003

Futuyma, Douglas J. **Evolution** Sinauer Associates, 2009

Lane, Nick The Vital Question: Why is Life the Way it is? Profile Books, 2016

Zimmer, Carl Evolution: The Triumph of an Idea William Heinemann, 2001

Geoffrey Ponder

Key Events in the Origin of the Chloroplast

This essay will consider the ways in which Chloroplasts have evolved to become an integral part of all plant and algal cells. Various theories have been proposed but it is now generally accepted that chloroplasts originated with the enveloping of cyanobacteria into another type of pharokyte cell. We will look at the ways in which a cyanobacteria could have entered into a pharokyte cell, and how the original cyanobacteria adapted so that it was able to further evolve the functions it plays within the cell.

Understanding the Evolution of Life

Usually we consider the term 'evolution' as applying to plants or animals, although arguably the term can have a much wider application. When considering biological life, this is certainly how Charles Darwin used the term. However the term can also be used when considering evolution of the actual cells which make up the physical content of any animal or plant. The evolution of cells covers literally billions of years, and has enabled cells to take on a wide variety of both form and function.

Here we will give particular attention to one aspect of the general evolution of cells, the original 'creation' of the chloroplasts which play a fundamental role in the life of plant and algal cells. This is a highly complex subject, given considerable attention since the beginning of the twentieth century, with key theories being formed since around 1960.

Theories of evolution are crucially important in explaining the form of virtually everything in life. It is due to incremental changes that specific features have evolved in both animals and plants. However there is a tendency for biologists to give the most attention to plants and animals as they currently exist, without giving due attention to the way they have evolved from earlier forms.

Nick Lane expressed concern about this in his book The Vital Question - Why is Life the Way it is? He argues strongly that there is great benefit in having a better understanding of how cells actually evolved, although admittedly there is still a great deal of speculation about this. Richard Dawkins, in A Devil's Chaplain, quotes Theodosius Dobzhanksy as saying "Nothing in biology makes sense except in the light of evolution".

When considering how evolution has taken place, there are various competing theories; with contributions from sciences such as biochemistry, chemistry, geology, ecology, phylogenetics and even cosmology. Over recent decades there has been much more genomic evidence to work from, with thousands of complete genomic sequences to help support specific theories.

It is hoped that if we gain a better understanding of how fundamental cells evolved in the first place, this will help give a better insight into how even more complex life forms also evolved over hundreds of thousands of years.

Overview of Chloroplasts and the Functions they perform

We are getting a better understanding of what chloroplasts actually are. They are an essential component in the functioning of plant cells (assuming from now on that when plants are referred to in relation to chloroplasts we will take the reference to apply to algal life as well).

A diagram of a typical Eukaryote cell is shown below. This has a number of important components, including mitochondria and chloroplasts. As it happens, it is thought that both organisms evolved to become key components of plant cells in a similar manner which will be considered later in this essay.

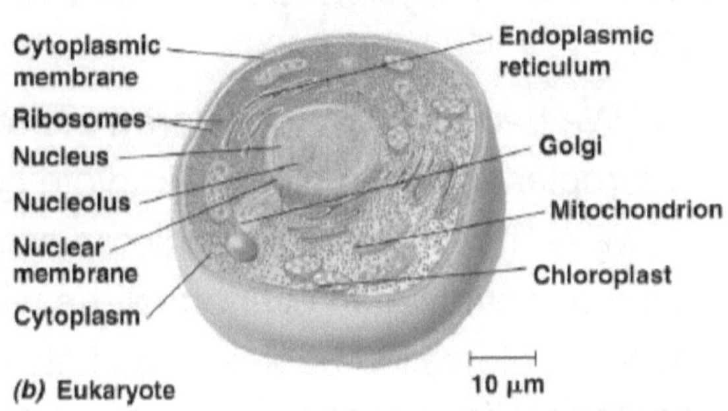

The main role of chloroplasts is to produce energy in forms that can be used by the cell which encloses them in the ongoing maintenance of life as well as continue growth. The energy is produced by a form of photosynthesis, making use of the photosynthetic pigment chlorophyll which is contained within the chloroplast. The chlorophyll captures energy from sunlight, and the energy is converted and stored in the molecules ATP and NADPH. The oxygen used is absorbed from water contained within the cell. The ATP and NADPH is then used to make organic molecules from Carbon

Dioxide: this process is known as the Calvin cycle.

Overview of Cyanobacteria as Prokaryote Cells

We had already considered the role that chloroplasts play in plant eukaryote cells. However it is thought that chloroplasts originally evolved in cyanobacteria which are basic single celled bodies. The field of bacteria is fascinating if for nothing else than the sheet metabolic diversity. Bacteria are able to perform a wide variety of biochemical functions, and different types can survive in the most hostile environments.

Cyanobacteria are one form of prokaryote cells which are much more basic, and evolved much earlier, than eukaryote cell. A diagram of a model prokaryote cell is shown below. You will see that there are fewer components in a typical prokaryote cell, and they do not function in as sophisticated a manner as a eukaryote cell.

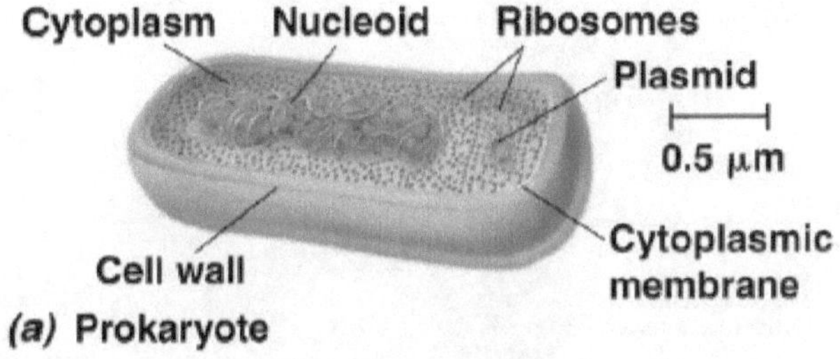

Cyanobacteria are sometimes caller blue-green algae, even they are more correctly single-cell prokaryotes. They obtain their energy from the sun via a process of photosynthesis. This is performed in distinctive folds in the outer membrane of the cell. The energy from the sunlight is used to split water molecules into oxygen, protons and electrons.

A diagram of a cyanobacteria is shown below. It is useful to compare this to the picture of a typical prokaryote cell above.

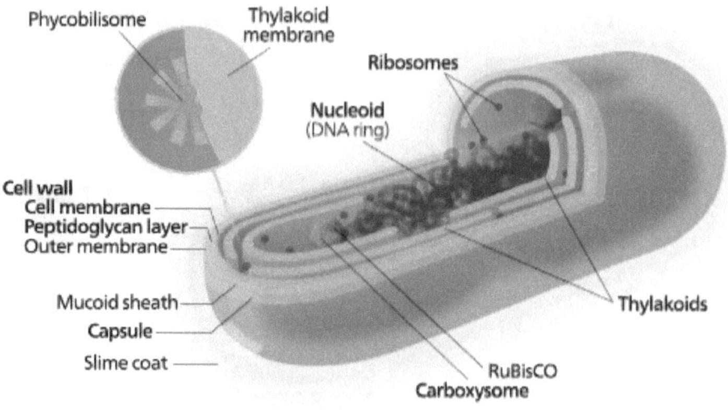

It is thought that the separation of oxygen by cyanobacteria is likely to have brought about the conversion of the early oxygen-poor environment of the earth to one which became steadily more oxygen-rich. The Great Oxygenation Event caused a 'rusting of the Earth', dramatically changing life forms and leading to the near-extinction of previously widespread anaerobic organisms.

The Penetration of Cyanobacteria into Eukaryote Cells

There is evidence that even before chloroplasts began to appear in eukaryote cells, mitochondria were already in place. These mitochondria were able to convert energy from various types of food present in the cell. Evidence for the prior existence of mitochondria is that all eukaryotes contain mitochondria, but only some have chloroplasts.

There have been various theories proposed about how chloroplasts came to exist in eukaryote cells. The theory now most commonly accepted by researchers is that chloroplasts are some kind of derivation from already existing cyanobacteria. For a start, chloroplasts are structurally similar to cyanobacteria. Both have a double membrane, and contain DNA, ribosomes and thylakoids. They are both small, round blue-green pigmented bodies that lack a nucleus. They both photosynthesise in a similar manner, and both assimilate carbon dioxide and proliferate by division.

This came about through a process of endosymbiosis, that is a cell living within another cell. Around a billion years ago a free-living cyanobacteria somehow entered an early eukaryote cell, already containing mitochondria, either as food or else as an internal parasite. Often it is suggested that the cyanobacteria was somehow 'engulfed' by the other cell. The cyanobacteria will have managed to escape the phagocytic vacuole it was contained in.

Here is a schematic diagram of Endosymbiosis

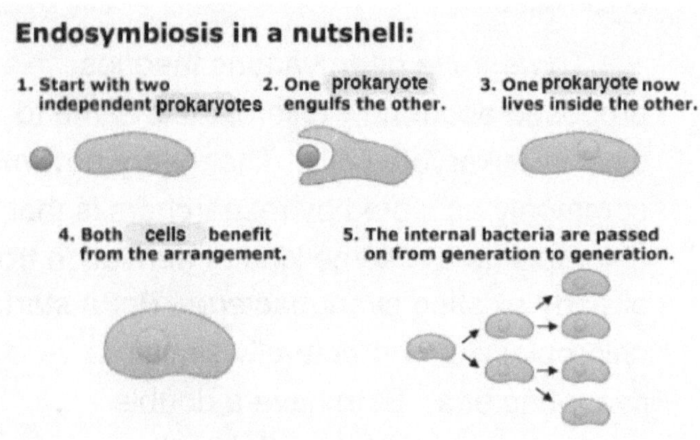

http://evolution.berkeley.edu

The new resident body within the eukaryote cell quickly became of benefit as it will have been providing food, allowing the ongoing presence of the intruder. Over time the cyanobacteria will have become more fully assimilated into the eukaryote, with many of its genes either being lost or else transferred into the nucleus of the host cell. It is possible that some of its proteins will have been synthesised in the cytoplasm of the host cell, and imported back into the invading body. By this stage the new presence in the host cell could be considered as a chloroplast rather than as a free-living cyanobacteria.

Curiously enough, it can be suggested that chloroplasts are still not fully integrated within plant cells. They still have some of their own DNA which will be involved in their replication in the cell, even though there is at most 10% of that typically found in a cyanobacteria. Molecular biologists are still not sure why their should be this residue, instead of chloroplasts taking full advantage of all the DNA contained within the nucleus of the eukaryote cell.

Even though there is general agreement that chloroplasts originated as cyanobacteria, there was still debate about whether chloroplasts came from a single endosymbiotic event, or else many independent engulfments across various eukaryotic lineages. Increasingly it is being accepted that most organisms with chloroplasts either share a single ancestor, or else they obtained their chloroplasts from organisms with an ancestor that took in a cyanobacteria between 600 and 1,600 million years ago. Admittedly, so far I have not seen any clearly argued case for this 'single-shot' proposal.

In summary, after a great deal of research and speculation over the years, we can now be confident about the way that chloroplasts evolved to be a key component in plant eukaryote cells. Along with the evolution of mitochondria, this twin evolution has been once of the factors which have enabled organisms to become multi-cellular, and helps to explain the complexity of life that we see all around us.

Works Referenced

Archibald, John **One plus One equals One** Oxford University Press, 2014

Dawkins, Richard **A Devil's Chaplain** Weidenfeld and Nicolson, 2003

Futuyma, Douglas J. **Evolution** Sinauer Associates, 2009

Lane, Nick **The Vital Question: Why is Life the Way it is?** Profile Books, 2016

Zimmer, Carl **Evolution: The Triumph of an Idea** William Heinemann, 2001

Evolution in Plants

The Making of Life from Chemicals

Although it would be considered to be extraordinary, plants and life generally can be said to have evolved out of basic chemical elements. Alexander Oparin and the evolutionist J.B.S Haldane separately proposed that life originated in a 'primeval soup' composed of organic molecules. In 1953 an experiment was performed with water, ammonia, methane and hydrogen being mixed in a glass apparatus. Heat, electrical sparks and a condenser were applied and the set up left to work away for a week.

At the end of this initial phase, over ten percent of the carbon in the mixture had become incorporated into organic compounds, with another two percent forming amino acids. This artificial environment synthesised thirteen of the twenty amino acids found in proteins. It had been proved that non-biological processes could produce most of the components which bring about life. Further investigations showed that amino acids, in similar experimental conditions, could link up into small protein fragments.

Although we can't be sure of the original conditions on earth, other experiments using different combinations of elements have also shown compatible results.

It is even possible that these vital substances could have been brought to earth from outer space. The Murchison meteorite, which impacted Australia in 1969, was found to contain various amino acids and other biologically relevant molecules. Similar analyses of meteorites elsewhere have added further evidence that basic life can be synthesised in extraterrestrial environments. This basic life could have been transferred to the surface of the early earth, and presumably since then, via meteorite impacts.

Although these chemicals cannot be said to make up life as such, nevertheless in the right atmospheric conditions very basic forms of life could have been formed from these elements.

What were the very first Predecessors of Plants?

If we go far back in the earth's history as far as 3 billion years ago the air was thick and acrid with clouds of volcanic activity, and there were shallow seas bordering on islands. The very first organisms were single-cell, of a microscopic size, and consisted of just a simple outer membrane with a few proteins inside. These were the earliest forms of bacteria. Over time these tiny cells merged together to form slimy layers covering the seabed.

Initially these bacteria needed to be able to absorb near-infrared light from the sun that penetrated the murky atmosphere. This light converted the carbon dioxide and hydrogen-based organic chemicals within the bacteria. Sulphates or sulphur were produced as a form of very basic nutrients. These basic chemical reactions, using energy from the sun, could be said to be the origin of plant life as we know it. This form of photosynthesis uses light energy to produce vital organic food for the bacterial cell.

Now that the bacteria were no longer dependent on absorbing energy from chemical scraps of nutrients in the sediment in the oceans, they were able to further evolve over a long period of time. The organic compounds and sugars which they were able to produce from photosynthesis enabled the bacteria to have both growth and movement.

A significant advance took place around 2.7 billion years ago when new cells appeared which are a progression on the most primitive form of bacteria. These new cells, cyanobacteria, have pigments which had evolved sufficiently so that they were able to absorb visible light which served to break down chemical compounds to produce food. As further evolution took place, a varied range of photosynthetic pigments developed, including a substance which is now more commonly known as chlorophyll.

The substances these more sophisticated pigments produced as a by-product were no longer just harsh sulphurous gases, but the very basic but highly productive molecule oxygen. These oxygen-generating cyanobacteria proved to be wonderfully productive in this early world and they formed large colonies consisting of many billions of cells. They were absorbing carbon dioxide from the sea, and converting this into oxygen, using light energy, which could them transfer into the atmosphere in large clouds.

The cyanobacteria are considered responsible for the so-called Great Oxidation Event which was to have a profound long-term effect on the early world. Strictly speaking cyanobacteria are not plants, but they enabled the first most basic forms of plant life to appear.

Around 1.6 billion years ago oxygen comprised about 10% of the earth's atmosphere. Various other forms of photosynthetic life had joined the cyanobacteria including red algae, brown algae and green algae. Over the next 500 million years these new forms continued to evolve, developing various adaptions which enabled them to survive more readily in a range of harsh environments. For instance, some algae developed multiple cells some of which could specialise in functions such as the production of energy and reproduction. Crucially some algae were able to package their genetic material into a single central nucleus.

These more developed algae can be said to be the first eukaryotic life forms, being predecessors of the more sophisticated cells that make up the modern forms of plant life. There were self-contained photosynthetic structures with green algae making up chloroplasts. At this stage the algae was still confined to watery environments as the algae needed to absorb water and nutrients from the immediate physical environment.

Around 500 million years ago the green algae began to be washed ashore and needed to be able to survive away from immediate contact with water, at least for short stretches of time. We can assume that over extended time these green algae further evolved so their dependence on direct contact with water gradually diminished.

Evolution of the first Plant Forms

The first forms of plant life could be said to be indicated by the development of reproductive spores in plants around 470 years ago. These spores, when examined, show tiny structures which resemble those seen in the very primitive plant forms that still exist and which we know as liverworts. Although liverworts are not confined to seas or lakes, nevertheless as they have no internal vascular system they rely on a moist external environment, and so have a limited range of sufficiently hospitable environments in which to grow.

Plankton is another form of bryophyte which still is found in all parts of our oceans today. Indeed, a single drop of water can contain many thousands of the free-floating organisms. Other forms of bryophytes are mosses, hornworts and liverworts. They are typically small, green and hair-like. Because their evolution has failed to properly enable them to transfer water between cells, they are restricted to dark and damp habitats. Nevertheless bryophytes are the third most diverse group of plants in the world, numbering well over 10,000 species.

Around 430 million years ago plants still have soft moist bodies and so found it difficult to survive in an open environment. Warm air caused the thin cell walls to quickly desicate. And water was still necessary for female gametes to combine with male gametes for reproduction.

It was necessary for further evolution to take place for algae to become more dessication-proof and survive more readily away from water.   The first land-based bryophytes developed root-like structures which provided some form of anchorage to the soil. Other enhancements were the development of more productive photosynthesis, and the ability to develop from limp origins to become tall and touch. Crucially they also needed to have greater reproductive success than their rivals.

More sophisticated plants forms have needed to be able to satisfy several prime needs. For a start, they need to be able to get water and nutrients to all the parts of the plant that are not in direct contact with the soil. Also the plant as a whole needs to be able to support itself so that it has a structure away from the buoancy of water.

The development of vascular plants was the need key stage in the overall evolution. An example if Cooksonia, dating from around 444 to 416 million years ago. These plants have an internal system of tubes to allow movement of water from below the ground up to raised parts of the plant. Water can be evenly distributed throughout the branching arms of the plant. This vascular structure is enabled by open-ended cells along the length of the stems. As a result, vital photosynthetic parts can survive to play their role in the life of the plant.

Over the next 400 million years vascular plant forms would continue to evolve giving rise to cycads, gingkos, ferns, conifers and eventually all the flower plants which presently occupy the earth. And all this from a limited range of chemicals in a harsh environment.

Works Referenced

Benson, Will **Kingdom of Plants - A Journey through their Evolution** Collins, 2012

King, John **Reaching for the Sun - How Plants Work** Cambridge University Press, 2011

Pallen, Mark **The Rough Guide to Evolution** Penguin Group, 2009

Zimmer, Carl **Evolution: The Triumph of an Idea** William Heinemann, 2001

Why we owe our Brains to Jellyfish

As fellow members of the species Homo Sapiens we tend to take great pride in our intellectual prowess. However I suggest that we all learn to be a little more modest. In future years sociologists and evolutionary scientists will look back at this Trumpian Age when we were forced to recognise the very real limitations to the sophistication of human thought processes.

I would like to play a part in this inevitable process of reevaluation, by proposing that however incredibly elaborate we like to think we are, we actually owe our brains to jellyfish! Let me explain.

How Brains needed to Evolve

Brains have needed to evolve for the same reason that all life forms have needed to evolve: to improve the competitiveness of sub-parts of any species. Any advantage a specific individual, or group of individuals have, means that the factors which enable it to have an advantage over others means it is more likely to breed the advantages into future generations.

Charles Darwin himself was more than curious about how animal brains have evolved over hundreds of millions of years, although he didn't understand how genetics works which would have given additional insights. He would have been aware that human brains have evolved from monkey brains which themselves have evolved from earlier species. It is even possible that he was aware of physical differences between monkey and human brains which enables the latter to be of greater cognitive processing and survival value.

Where did the Evolution of Brains Begin?

Darwin was also aware that the evolution of humans can be traced right back to the most primitive creatures, via the so-called tree of life. When considering the process of evolution over an extended period it makes sense to try to determine the initial most basic life forms from which our brains can be said to have evolved.

You can't get more basic that the creatures which make up the Coelenterates (sponges, jellyfish, etc) family. And, to be honest, 150 years ago many scientists would have concluded that these creatures don't actually have any kind of brain. However they do exhibit some kinds of behaviour in particular environmental conditions which indicate that they are able to 'think' or at least 'react' in some way or other.

It makes sense that extensive investigations have been made into the primitive sensory systems of Coelenterates. And sponges, however primitive looking, seem to be able to react to changes in their environment. Wilkinson (2015) has made some topical investigations here. Look as hard as we might, we are not able to see any nerves, muscles or sense organs in sponges. And about the only action they can perform is to filter micro-organisms, mainly bacteria, from seawater. So sponges, which date from around 770 to 850 million years ago can probably justify the requirement to indicate the most primitive origins of brain evolution.

Sponges are capable of very simple and slow body movements, although it is necessary to use time-delay photography to actually see any spatial change. For instance, they are able to contract parts of the body which has the effect of expelling food debris from their area of consumption.

But what brings about this movement, however painstakingly slow it appears to us? Well, it is obvious that the sponges are not able to observe anything, either visually or by touch. However it seems that they nevertheless somehow respond to changes in their immediate physical environment. Sally Leys has found that if certain chemicals such as glutamate are brought to the sponge, then contractions can be induced, even virtual spasms if the chemical is particularly concentrated.

Significantly, glutamate is one of the chemicals which are found at synapses of the nerves of more complex animals, serving as neurotransmitters. This would suggest that animals that have evolved from sponges have inherited the capacity to use glutamate to function as an essential part of their neural systems.

Why Jellyfish can be said to be the originators of our Brains

If sponges can't be said to have any kind of brain, then what is the animal further down the tree of evolution that can be said to have a brain? Well, strictly speaking, jellyfish don't have brains, but they do have more sophisticated neural systems which can be said to be the immediate precursors of brains.

There has been ongoing research on the neural systems of jellyfish for well over a hundred years, and it might seem curious that definitive conclusions on the fully story on how they work have yet to emerge. Partly this is due to the difficulty in finding physiological elements in jellyfish which are either very small, or virtually invisible because of their transparency. Increasingly sophisticated microscopes helped with the first problem, and over an extended period more effective staining techniques were developed which better revealed significant traces.

One of the scientists who played an important role in research on the neural system of jellyfish was George Romanes. He was admitted to Gonville and Caius College at Cambridge in July 1867, initially intent on studying to be a clergyman. However he decided instead to read the natural sciences tripos, graduating with a Class B (while Francis Darwin, son of Charles, graduated with a Class A in the same year). As it was, Charles Darwin also undertook theological studies at Cambridge before, fortunately, concentrating full time on scientific pursuits.

There was plenty in the field of physiology to attract his interest. He became aware of the rhythmic contractions of the jellyfish bell which cause movement in a specific direction. This was one of the observations that aroused an interest in physiology research seen from an evolutionary perspective, particularly the development of a nervous system.

At the time another prominent researcher, Agassiz, had determined that "no nervous system has yet been discovered in Medusae", although fine fibres running along the margin of the swimming bell had been detected. Romans set about finding whether nerves actually existed in jellyfish.

One of the problems was that jellyfish lack organs that could be used to indicate attachments to nerve cells. For a time Romanes recognised the possibility that a distinctive nervous system had not developed and so was not to be found. However he nevertheless proposed that "In its simplest and probably earliest form, a nerve is nothing more than a thin strand of irritable protoplasm ..". In this case, there was no need to locate any kind of central 'brain' but instead concentrate on identifying what kind of electrical message was being transmitted by the nerves.

In his research, Romanes used several fundamental methods. He would test conductivity with mechanical and electrical stimulation. He would make elaborate cuts through the bell and the 'locomotor centres' and see what effects these would have. And he tested for the effects of drugs already known to stimulate the nerve and muscle cells of higher animals. Cutting into the bell had interesting effects as often excitation would still spread which would not be expected if the nerves were considered to have the nature of discrete fibres.

In 1876 Romanes was able to report distinctive conclusions, such as "… in animals which, as we have seen from other evidence, present us with the first indications of a nervous system … (appearing) to have already undergone a differentiation of its functions … capable not only of influencing contiguous contractile parts, but also of being influenced by distant excitable parts".

So although Romanes was not able to show that jellyfish have brains, he nevertheless proved that the nerve systems of jellyfish are further evolved from anything existing in sponges. He had observed that the nerve net in jelly fish is the first evolutionary manifestation of an organised nervous system. The nerve systems of jellyfish are much more sophisticated than earlier thought and can be considered the next best thing to a central electrical signal processing unit (or brain).

These findings must have thrilled Darwin as both he and Thomas Huxley recognised the importance of the jellyfish investigations for evolutionary theory. They actively encouraged Romanes in his research, and Darwin served as a kind of father figure to his younger scientific colleague.

In his turn, Romanes published **Animal Intelligence** in 1882, and **Mental Evolution in Animals** in 1883. He explicitly served tribute to Darwin in 1886 with **Physiological Selection: An Additional Suggestion to the Origin of Species**. Ironically he died of a brain tumour in 1894.

Wrapping up Remarks

So it looks like we owe a great deal of gratitude to the humble jellyfish. The next time I treat myself to a seaside holiday, if it comes about that while I'm out on the water I notice a friendly jellyfish drifting past, I'll nod in it's direction, out of respect, while feeling the warmth of the sun on my body, doing my best to imitate its languorous movement, while pondering the plans I need to make for the next Evolution class at Madingley Hall.

Works Referenced

Anctil, Michel **Dawn of the Neuron - The Early Struggles to trace the Origin of Nervous Systems** McGill-Queen's University Press, 2015

Pallen, Mark **The Rough Guide to Evolution** Penguin Group, 2009

Wilkinson, Matt **Restless Creatures - The Story of Life in Ten Movements** (hardback edition) Icon Books, 2016

Zimmer, Carl **Evolution: The Triumph of an Idea** William Heinemann, 2001

The Evolution of Polyps

When considering evolution, there is still plenty of interest in basic organisms such as polyps, even though they have hardly evolved for hundreds of millions of years. Also with polyps there are important connections with the geology of substantial parts of mother earth.

In this paper I will first be describing polyps, and how they function in every day life. Then I will consider ways in which they have evolved to become as adapted are reasonably possible to fit into their natural environment.

The role that polyps play in the development of coral reefs will be covered. And the prospects for the future in respect to both polyps and coral reefs will be discussed. As you will see, the outlook is not particularly good.

Description of Polyps

Polyps are coelenterates, and can be considered anthozoans, a kind of mixture of animal and plant. They are part of the group cnidarians which also includes freshwater hydras, and other sea anemones, corals and jellyfish. They are not particularly impressive to look at. As Dawkins (2016) succinctly puts it, ".. they are radially symmetrical around a central mouth, with no obvious head, no front or rear, no right or left, only an up or down."

Alternatively it can be said that they are basically a roundish bag with a mouth, and usually a number of tentacles around the mouth, mostly inside. Their life is spent fixed to a coral base, and they are not able to move at all. They have no brain, but instead a basic nerve network around the mouth. To eat they bring water-borne particles into their mouths using their tentacles, and waste is ejected by the same route. Plankton is particularly popular for eating, although other basic items can be digested as well. Incidentally they usually eat at night when their exposed tentacles are less likely to be attacked by other predators.

Although there are some solitary species of polyps, generally they gather in large groups and live in mutually supportive colonies. In some cases there can be connective thin tissue between polyps. It is key that for nearly all polyps they can only live in warm shallow water.

Depending on the species, polyps can breed in various ways. Sometimes small buds can develop on the exterior of polyps and these differentiate themselves from the original polyp. More commonly they replicate themselves by pushing large amounts of eggs and sperm into the surrounding water. It has been observed that this tends to take place with many polyps acting at the same time, suggesting that there is a higher chance of survival of offspring if any predator is overwhelmed by the density of reproductive material.

A fundamental aspect of polyp life is the symbiosis with algae which is a key to their evolutionary success. Colonies of polyps are found to have single-cell algae, in the form of dinoflagellates which are microscopical, actually growing in the coral tissue itself. These algae are called zooxanthellae and actually live in the endoderm of coral polyps as well as any tissue that connects polyps in a reef colony.

How does this symbiosis actually work? The algae efficiently produce energy from sunlight through a process of photosynthesis. This enables the polyp's tissues to deposit beneath themselves calcium carbonate in a fiber-like crystalline form called aragonite. So the coral tissues are able to lay down a skeleton of limestone, creating their own substrate which in turn develops into extensive reefs. In their turn, algal cells use the carbon dioxide respired by the coral tissue to produce oxygen and the carbohydrates which are used by the coral.

Algal densities can reach millions of cells per square centimetre of coral tissue. The zooxanthellae are critically important for the production of the massive amounts of limestone deposited to make up the reefs. So in effect the polyp animals are working with the plant algae to produce extensive geological structures.

Finally it is worth noting that thousands of species of coral have been described - sea whips, sea fans, domes, brains, organ pipes and many others. This, of course, is one of the main reasons that coral reefs have such an attraction for visitors. And, interestingly enough, most can mate with close relatives to make new hybrid forms.

The Evolutionary Success of Polyps

All creatures need to evolve so that they become adapted to their particular environment. This is certainly true of polyps, although it seems they have hardly evolved in hundreds of millions of years indicating that their adaptation is near enough as good as it is going to get. Having said that, there is a new condition which threatens the balance which will be discussed later in more detail.

The earliest polyps appeared towards the end of the Precambrian period, and around three hundred million years ago coral edifices began to look rather like they do today. It can be argued that polyps were one of the natural features that helped Darwin consolidate his theories on evolution. His first book (apart from those recounting his travels around the world) was on coral reefs, written around 1842.

Providing environmental conditions are suitable for their way of life, polyps are very successful in both living and spreading. In some parts of the world, such as the Great Barrier Reef, coral reefs in effect 'built' by polyps extend for many hundreds of miles along the coast. Admittedly the water temperature needs to be warm, but not too warm, and because a suitable level of salinity is required for their effective functioning, polyps are not found where rivers open into the sea.

They can be vulnerable to predators, and some types of fish have developed mouths which are specialised in extracting polyps from their reef attachment. More serious however is the occasional overwhelming conquest by Crown of Thorns starfish, which for still unknown reasons will rise out of the depths of the oceans in large numbers and cause extensive damage to the edible parts of coral reefs. The starfish then retreat to the depths allowing the reefs to gradually recover until the next conquest.

There is also competition between corals for prescious space on the reefs, with various different species of coral involved. Dominant forms of polyps can release deadly toxins which destroy nearby polyps. More aggressive polyps can even exude mesenterial filaments onto neighbouring polyps which will be digested leaving little remaining after a few hours. Also long sweeper tentacles can be extended, much longer than those typically used for the ingestion of foods. Admittedly these assertive actions require the expenditure of large amounts of energy, indicating the importance of being able to obtain further space on existing reefs.

Although life can be difficult for polyps, they can be said to be virtually immortal as they are able to renew cloned versions of themselves almost without limit from special cells. And there are records of individual polyps surviving for more than a hundred years.

Finally, the importance of symbiotic relationships for polyps needs to be mentioned. We have already revealed the close relationships they have with algae which enable the reefs to steadily develop. Also many sea creatures are very dependent on the reefs which polyps have brought about as a suitable environment in which to live, eat, breed, and survive. Coral reefs form an extensive colony for a wide range of both animals and plants, and it is suggested that there are more fish species inhabiting reefs than anywhere else in the oceans.

The Importance of Polyp-Made Coral Reefs

We have already mentioned that Charles Darwin took a particular interest in corals on his exploratory voyage around the world. This interest was his finding, following on from his geological mentor Lyell, sea shells embedded in extensive masses of limestone high in some mountains such as the Andes.

Darwin accepted Lyell's conclusions that at distant times the surface of the earth had buckled in various places raising areas which had previously been below sea level thousands of meters into the air. On the other hand, if the sea level in a particular area was dropping, then the corals would continue growing upwards so they would remain just below the surface, building mountain ranges underwater as it were.

So how are the coral reefs actually formed? For a start the location needs to be off-shore from the mainland, in warm waters of a suitable salinity. Also there is a requirement for a photic zone where there is plenty of sunlight. The development needs to be close to the surface as most coral building polyps can only flourish in the topmost levels of seawater. The polyps cover previously developed areas of coral reef, in effect making up a thin veneer of flesh no thicker than a jar of jam spread over each square meter. Incidentally, the coral reefs can be said to be related to ancient stromatolites originally produced by cyanobacteria.

Evolution has given the polyp reef-builders the ability to extract dissolved marine chemicals and turn them into stone. Special cells on the polyp's surface are used to pump ions of calcium, with their positive electrical charge, from the sea into the cell. The photosynthesizing dinoflagellates within the polyps pull carbon dioxide from the sky and combine it with calcium. As a result, limestone, a very pure form of calcium carbonate, forms the reef structure which can be vast. Coral is an alliance of carbon with calcium and oxygen, as are all plants and animals.

Just the chemical processing is impressive. The polyps are able to lay down carbon at almost twice the rate of a rain forest, although strong sunlight is required as three times the amount of coral is produced in the light than in the dark. There is an enormously high rate of protein production as a side effect, which is important for the feeding of people harvesting the fish living around the reefs. Arguably shallow-watered tropical reefs are the most productive natural places on the earth.

So the coral-building power of polyps is certainly a key factor in the maintenance of many forms of life on earth. However this existence is under threat, as we will see in the last section of this paper.

The Future for Polyps and their Coral Reefs?

However well they have evolved up to this particular position in the history of the world, the future outlook for polyps is not good. As Sheppard (2014) points out, "Coral reefs as a whole have been described as being the canaries in the coal mine - they are the part of the ecosystem that will be the first to succumb to overexploitation and abuse".

Jones (2007) is referring to polyps when he writes "… their plight warns us that unless we mend our ways our own future is gloomy indeed." And his book, titled simply "Coral", is tellingly subtitled "A Pessimist in Paradise".

The fundamental problem is the likelihood of global warming, despite many people including senior political leaders of major global powers scoffing at this concern. Polyps are sensitive to higher temperatures, and cannot survive in warmer waters for extended periods.

Any symbiotic relationship is disturbed by environmental stress, and under difficult conditions the polyps will expel their inherent algal cells, or the algal cells will die off by themselves. Temporary disruption is not necessarily so serious, and polyps can regenerate where earlier they had died off. However after extreme stress, the entire coral will die.

Living coral is wonderful partly because of the spectacular colours of the pigments in the algal cells used for energy photosynthesis. The actual polyps are relatively transparent, so if the algal cells are disappearing then the white limestone beneath the polyps will show through with a bleached appearance. This bleaching effect is happening more frequently in recent years, and is likely to worsen if sea temperatures continue to rise.

And the problem is not just the loss of colour. With the decrease in polyp life constantly generating new coral, the now 'dead' coral tends to break up and degenerate into sand. The foreshore of the nearby land becomes exposed to the full strength of waves, often resulting in erosion. There is long-term damage to important and sophisticated ecosystems. Fish numbers and variety quickly decrease off causing local, usually poor, communities to suffer from reduced seafood availability. Tourist and scuba diver numbers drop away, removing an important source of income for these communities.

No wonder many people are so concerned about signs of coral bleaching. Ideally polyps would adapt to higher sea temperatures, and evolve new coping mechanisms. Unfortunately we do not live in an ideal world.

Works Referenced

Dawkins, Richard and Wong, Yan **The Ancestor's Tale - A Pilgrimage to the Dawn of Life** Weidenfeld & Nicolson, 2016

Jones, Steve **Coral - A Pessimist in Paradise** Abacus, 2014

Pallen, Mark **The Rough Guide to Evolution** Penguin Group, 2009

Sheppard, Anne **Coral Reefs - Secret Cities of the Sea** Natural History Museum, 2016

Sheppard, Charles **Coral Reefs - A Very Short Introduction** Oxford University Press, 2014

Sheppard, Charles R.C., Davy, Simon K. and Pilling, Graham M. **The Biology of Coral Reefs** Oxford University Press, 2012

The Evolution of Human Diversity

When Charles Darwin developed his theories relating to Evolution, the principal way that he considered all living beings, both plant and animal, to have evolved was through Natural Selection. However it is increasingly being recognised that other factors play an important role in evolution. These can be termed 'random' or 'non-adaptive' causes.

Evolution has played a crucial role in key aspects of human diversification. This is obviously of fundamental interest to evolutionary scientists. It helps that most of the major parts of human diversification have taken place over the past 50,000 years, and there is plenty of evidence available for the development of relevant theories.

In this paper I have several main aims. The first is to discuss many of the key aspects of Natural Selection and indicate why it has been so crucial in the course of biological evolution over several billion years.

In addition I will cover some of the many ways by which random evolution takes place, with particular attention given to the role it has played in human evolution. Another section will outline a history of the evolution of modern man, allowing insights into how random events have influenced this progression and diversification.

The paper will end with a discussion of the effects that non-adaptive evolution is having in the modern world, and potential ongoing effects.

Natural Selection in Evolution

Natural selection is one of the most fascinating aspects of modern science. Indeed the philosopher Daniel Dennett, in his book Darwin's Dangerous Ideas (1995) claimed that natural selection is the best idea that anyone had ever had. "In a single stroke, the idea of evolution by natural selection unifies the realm of life, meaning, and the purpose with the realm of space and time, cause and effect, mechanism and physical law".

The ongoing forces of natural selection allow for the gradual better adaptation to prevailing conditions, and account for the endless diversity of life. Life's attributes result from inherited differences in the chances of passing on selected genes. For organisms to adapt to a new environment, some mutations must increase the chances of survival and reproduction of their carriers.

On any study of natural life it is apparent that there is an ongoing struggle for existence. The chances of survival, or the gradual development of more effective adaptations, will tend to lead to the greater preservation of any particular species, and so be most likely to be inherited by offspring. These variations can be very slight and due to a wide range of causes.

With evolution over time, offspring will have a better chance of surviving as many individuals are regularly born but only a limited number will live to produce more of a similar genetic type. Any slight variation in the genes of a plant or animal will tend to be preserved. At the same time, nature tends to be very wasteful with most organisms producing far more offspring than can possibly survive.

It is a fundamental advantage if a range of variants can be produced at any stage so that natural selection is able to tend to favour any variants which are of greater value to the long-term survival of the species. Having said this, there is no sense of logic in natural selection: the development of a wide range of cancers is proof of this.

To get a better overall understanding of natural selection, it is worth considering some of the different types which can be said to be functioning in the real world.

For a start there is 'stabilising selection' which has the effect of removing genetic diversity from the population. This is selection again extreme values for a given character trait, having the effect of maintaining an adaptive average. Life can be said to be a trade-off between the costs and benefits of a trait, and conservative forces in effect thwart deviations in form or function. This explains why some distinctive morphologies have varied little over millions of years. For instance, dogs can be bred to vary widely in many different traits, looking completely unlike each other, yet wolves and foxes remain pretty much the same over many generations.

Then there is 'directional selection' where natural selection favours a phenotype at one extreme of the current range of variation. For instance, when bacteria are exposed to antibiotics, directional selection will tend to drive the species population to become steadily more resistant. When overfishing is taking place, there is a tendency for small fish to survive better than large as they are less likely to be caught. Directional selection has the effect of driving an organism's evolution when it is introduced to a new environment or new ecological niche.

Disruptive selection is where individuals at the extremes of a character distribution are preferred over those closer to the average. For instance, this can take place when forms of camouflage need to be developed. The term 'sympatric speciation' is used when disruptive evolution is believed to be the driving force behind the birth of a new species in the same location.

And 'balancing selection' is where genetic variation is maintained within a population via a number of different mechanisms. An individual can be said to have hererozygotic advantage if it has two different versions of a gene over individual species which have two identical versions of the particular gene.

'Frequency-dependent selection' is where the more common a particular characteristic is, the more it tends to be selected against. An example of this is the profusion of human tissue types which have been driven by the actions of infectious micro-organisms.

So this section of the paper had the intention of outlining some of the key basic principles of natural selection. The next section points out some of the crucial differences with 'random' evolution' where non-adaptive selection gives a better understanding of how particular features tend to evolve.

The Role of Random or Chance Selection

The previous section covered the most 'traditional' form of evolution, natural selection. Now it is the turn of 'random', or 'chance', or non-adaptive evolution to be covered.

For a start, we need a better understanding of the word 'chance' when applied to evolution as this is critically important. Chance implies that there is no specific purpose behind an event, no logical explanation for the occurrence of an outcome. It can be said that scientists do not consider any natural phenomena to be purposeful. Having said that, the outcome of a circumstance is more definable for adaptive evolution than it is for non-adaptive evolution. At least there is some degree of predictability of the outcome when various alternatives are being selected for.

Chance, or randomness, means that when physical causes can result in any of several outcomes, the outcome in any event cannot be predicted in advance as there is no identifiable advantage in any particular outcome.

There are various types of chance effects in evolution. One of the most important is Random Genetic Drift where important random processes are taking place. These include genetic mutation and random fluctuations in the frequencies of alleles or haplotypes. Random Genetic Drift tends to happen where natural populations are finite in size. Old alleles can be replaced by new ones through random fluctuations in frequencies. The significance of such chance events in evolution is admittedly often uncertain.

Another type of chance effect is known as Bottlenecks. There can be a reduction in population numbers due to killings, disease, or movement of sub-groups. In this case, individuals close to each other usually share the same genes. If a population goes through a period of reduced numbers, a so-called bottleneck, only the genes of the survivors will persist. Their descendants will then be genetically different from the population before the bottleneck occurred. In these cases, genes can be traced back to a limited number of original people. The result is usually much higher rates of gene-related diseases than found typically. This itself can cause further loss of genetic variability.

Another cause of non-adaptive evolution can be due to so-called Founder effects, sometimes known as peripatric speciation. These are where a new population is established by a small number of colonists, sometimes as few as a single mating pair. It is likely that some rarer alleles will not have been carried by the founders, and if the population remains small then genetic variation will be limited. When founder effects are combined with genetic drift, the effect can be to ensure reproductive isolation from the original population.

There are various examples of founder effects in different parts of the world. For example, originally limited numbers of Afrikaner people would have migrated from the Netherlands to South Africa. This has resulted in certain genetic defects found more commonly in Afrikaner people than would otherwise be expected.

Similarly Australian aborigines have low heterozygosity, that it variability in their genetic inheritance. This can be attributed to the relatively low numbers involved in the original settlement into Australia around

60,000 years ago. By contrast, Africa is the most genetically variable continent, due to it being the original source of human populations around the world. Typically, as humans spread there is a corresponding loss of genetic variability.

In more recent discussions of non-adaptive speciation, explanations are given for how new biological species could have arisen.

Allopatric speciation is where geographic separation is a prerequisite, and population movements, destruction of an intervening population, and/or new geographic barriers mean that species become reproductively isolated.

Alternatively, parapatric speciation is where two diverging populations occupy and adapt to separate zones but come into contact at the boundary between the two zones. Sympatric speciation is where populations diverge into species while inhabiting the same locality: this can be accompanied by divergence in breeding times. And sympatric speciation is where new species form even when occupying the same location.

So random, or chance, or non-adaptive selection can give alternative understandings to explain the wide variety of species, and particularly human diversification.

How have Human Populations Diversified?

We have considered some of the reasons humans have diversified: now we can review some of the forms and outcomes of diversification to see how various types of selection have taken place.

Fortunately humans are good subjects for studying the effects of demographic accidents. A major problem for scientists when studying evolution is that too often any remaining evidence is very limited, and it is difficult to draw firm conclusions about how specific types of evolution actually came about. However for humans the historical records are relatively good. This is partly because we (the human race) have colonised various parts of the world relatively recently. As a kind of information proof of this, very often these restricted 'invasions' can be seen in the limited number of surnames found within a particular local community.

So what is meant by human diversity: in what ways have humans diversified over the last 50,000 or 100,000 years? For a start, humans can vary greatly in physical appearance. For instance, different groups can tend to be taller/shorter, fatter/thinner, with longer limbs, varied complexions, and so on. Also the form of physical movement has probably greatly changed over the years, and even now some people will probably claim that different races tend to move in distinctive ways.

Locations typically occupied can vary as well. For instance, people of a lighter complexion tend to be found in more northern countries, and even though they can survive easily enough in warmer climates they don't cope with strong sunlight so well. Also while most people tend to remain in the same general location, others particularly the 'hunter-gatherer' groupings, often need to move where food can be found most readily.

When considering human diversification over an extended period then social evolution can probably be considered to be the most crucial factor. It can be said that our more chimplike ancestors would have had more chimplike social lives. However as humans became more distinctly different, then this went along with the development of bigger brains, intelligence, mastery of language and took making skills. Actually Wallace, Darwin's co-evolutionist, had decided that our oversized brains are far more powerful than necessary and (as proposed in the last section of this paper) this might eventually result in our evolutionary downfall.

It is possible that as humans became more socially sophisticated, there was actually greater competition for mates, and the struggle for reproductive success became more challenging than ever. Undoubtedly humans will have needed to learn to live more harmoniously most of the time with the nearest social grouping, and learn how to hunt and defend more successfully. Also it will have been necessary for humans to teach and learn from each other, such as in areas of technical sophistication such as using tools.

However we need to recognise that at a basic level we have a great deal in common with the great apes. Indeed, bone for bone we are almost identical. Our gene sets are similar as well. Darwin had concluded that man evolved from gorillas and chimpanzees, and because these animals were originally based in Africa then it is likely that man had evolved originally in the same area. It now appears likely that all humans on the planet evolved from just a few thousand Africans.

The continued evolution of man resulted in ever greater diversification in ways of living and achievements. The invention of the first stone tools was around 2.5 million years ago. A million years later the crude blades were fashioned into massive hand axes. Around half a million years ago man learned how to master fire. DNA evidence indicates that the first modern humans evolved around 200,000 years ago, although the actual times might be a bit arbitrary. And 50,000 years ago we began painting on cave walls, carving jewelry, making intricate weapons, and performing elaborate burials.

There are substantial findings of Neanderthal remains from around 200,000 to 30,000 years ago. However it would seem that the earliest Cro-Magnon Europeans were significantly more sophisticated than the Neanderthals, and probably didn't evolve from that sub-species. It is possible that the greater sophistication of Cro-Magnons with superior fighting skills resulted in the extinction of the Neanderthal people.

So humans have diversified greatly over an extended period of time, as well as further diversified to a lesser extent in different geographical locations around the world. We can take it for granted that all the various aspects of diversification can be considered to be the outcome of evolution, both adaptive and random.

Are there non-Random Limits to Human Diversity?

To finish off this paper on human evolution, I make some suggestions that need to be considered on a very tentative basis.

Over the extent of life on earth, selection tends to take place when more individuals are born than there are resources available to support them. Even today this is the situation for many people in the Third World. However are we now seeing unnatural levels of genetic modification?

In the modern age we arguably have distorted evolution. What are some examples of this? In the western world people are being assisted to survive who otherwise would have died. In some cases, birth control is used to limit the number of children for parents who otherwise would have had more. There is some degree of selection of sex of babies, and increasingly genetic analysis is used to ensure that children will be reasonably healthy. Parents who know they have less desirable genes sometimes will limit their reproduction.

Previously it was the case that more materially successful people tended to have more children than people who could not provide the same level of nutritional support: now is the reverse more commonly the case? In rich countries such as Germany, France, Scandinavia, Japan, even China it would seem that national population numbers are dropping. Elsewhere in the world this is not so.

Previously overpopulation resulted in reduction of numbers at times of food shortage. Now often food is brought in to maintain life in people who would otherwise have died. It is extraordinary that in some cases people are being actively encouraged to have more children even though the expected quality of their upbringing won't necessarily be so desirable. It is much easier now for large numbers of people to move to new territories, as we are seeing with the transfer of economic refugees to areas where the quality of life is better.

What will be the implications of these developments? Certainly in terms of evolution and human diversity there are interesting days ahead!

Works Referenced

Dennet, Daniel **Darwin's Dangerous Idea - Evolution and the Meanings of Life**, Simon and Schuster 1996

Futuyma, Douglas J. **Evolution (Second Edition)** Sinauer Associates, 2009

Jones, Steve **Y - The Descent of Men** Abacus, 2003

Jones, Steve, Martin, Robert and Pilbeam, David **The Cambridge Encyclopaedia of Human Evolution** Cambridge University Press 1994

Pallen, Mark **The Rough Guide to Evolution** Penguin Group, 200

9Springer, Chris and Andrews, Peter **The Complete World of Human Evolution** Thames & Hudson, 2014

ABOUT THE AUTHOR

Geoffrey Ponder has a keen personal interest in various fields of Science, particularly Evolution and Genetics. Having already studied at three universities in the past, he was fortunate to complete a Diploma in Biological Evolution at Madingley Hall, part of Cambridge University, in July 2017.